T0039963

Also by Christopher Reid

POETRY

Arcadia

Pea Soup

Katerina Brac

In the Echoey Tunnel

Expanded Universes

For and After

Mr Mouth

The Song of Lunch

Nonsense

Six Bad Poets

The Curiosities

POETRY FOR CHILDREN

All Sorts

Alphabicycle Order

ANTHOLOGIES

Sounds Good: 101 Poems to Be Heard

Not to Speak of the Dog: 101 Short Stories in Verse

AS EDITOR

Letters of Ted Hughes

A SCATTERING

AND

ANNIVERSARY

A SCATTERING

AND

ANNIVERSARY

Christopher Reid

FARRAR, STRAUS AND GIROUX

NEW YORK

Farrar, Straus and Giroux
175 Varick Street, New York 10014

Published in 2017 by Farrar, Straus and Giroux
First paperback edition, 2018

Grateful acknowledgment is made for permission to reprint
A Scattering, originally published by Areté Books in 2009, and
Anniversary, originally published by Enitharmon Press in 2015.

The Library of Congress has cataloged the hardcover edition as follows:
Names: Reid, Christopher, 1949– author. | Reid, Christopher, 1949–
Scattering. | Reid, Christopher, 1949– Anniversary.
Title: A scattering and Anniversary / Christopher Reid.
Description: First edition. | New York : Farrar, Straus and Giroux, 2017.
Identifiers: LCCN 2017001323 | ISBN 9780374254261 (hardcover) |
ISBN 9780374716356 (e-book)
Classification: LCC PR6068.E426 A6 2017 | DDC 821/.914—dc23
LC record available at https://lccn.loc.gov/2017001323

Paperback ISBN: 978-0-374-53808-8

Designed by Quemadura

Our books may be purchased in bulk for promotional,
educational, or business use. Please contact your local
bookseller or the Macmillan Corporate and Premium Sales
Department at 1-800-221-7945, extension 5442, or by
e-mail at MacmillanSpecialMarkets@macmillan.com.

www.fsgbooks.com
www.twitter.com/fsgbooks
www.facebook.com/fsgbooks

Contents

A SCATTERING

(2009)

ANNIVERSARY
(2015)

A SCATTERING

(2009)

THE FLOWERS OF CRETE

Blessed by the indifference of the creatures—
big, sting-toting insects on haphazard reconnaissance,
scampering ants with their matching shadows
    scampering under them,
the squeaky-wheel bird in some tree, and the one
with the white throat and flight
    full of flusters and feints—
we take our breakfast of coffee and yoghurt out in the sun.

Even the sun, that more dangerous beast, has begun
his morning prowl in a spirit of negligent generosity,
not seeming to mind, or to want to murder us, much,
but laying the landscape out in its ancient
    shapes and colours,
velvety ochres and greens on the steep hill,
    a blue-green
glaze on the bay, as if to say,
'These are my wares. Yours more or less for the asking.
Of course I accept your paltry currency, your small change
    of days and hours.'

Bad old habit, but—
    because we're in Crete,
I find myself doubling
the Minotaur
in his puzzle-lair
    (now the scarcely troubling
    rumour of a rumour)
with an immediate threat:
    your skulking sarcoma.

The first was dispatched
    by a trick with a ball of string;
the second cannot be reached
    by medical science.
Yet it seems its defiance
has been met and matched
by yours, allowing
    respite, if not reprieve, and
two weeks with friends on this island.

Glib analogies!
Makeshift rhymes!

Please pardon the crimes
    of your husband the poet,
as he mazes the pages
of his notebook, in pursuit
    of some safe way out.

A man with long garment
is playing guitar
in a field full of birds,
horns of consecration
and double-axes.

The instrument
seems more a wonky lyre,
as I lean towards
the brushed decoration
on a small clay pyxis.

What it depicts is
beyond translation,
beyond words.
Exultantly peculiar.
A charmed moment.

Is there anything more absurd
than the Englishman abroad,
with his Panama hat and his hay fever
    firing off left, right and centre,
and his scraps of misremembered Classical Greek—
which, anyway, only ghosts of old schoolmasters speak
    and is useless in this place?
With his faltering tongue,
and his voluble nose,
and his roasted face
under the brim of that hat—
do you suppose
    there is anything more absurd
        than that?

But is there anything more sublime
than the Englishman's wife,
who is willing to climb
    the rockiest, thorniest slope
with abundant hope
in her heart, and an illustrated
Flowers of Crete in her hand,
    bloom-sleuthing for hours,

until she has chased
to its least accessible hiding-place,
then annotated,
    every specimen
        listed therein?

While he perspires
under that dapper
but ineffectual brim,
    and sneezes loudly, and sneezes loudly again,
the Englishman admires
his intrepid wife
and, somewhere in his brain,
begins to compose
a snatch of holiday doggerel:
    his humble, privately hummable
        rap rhapsody or hymn.

You could read this ruin
as the doubtful translation
of an epic, now largely lost.

A dry sort of pleasure,
discriminating, high-minded—
but not much to do with poetry.

The gist, the ground-plan,
is laid out in a light
parsimonious with shadow.

Like some antique board game
minus counters and rule book,
so no telling how the moves went round.

Where visible, the conjectures
and tinkerings of scholars
seem obtrusive, unhelpful.

You don't want their botched text.
You want the breath, pulse and footfall
of the girl who dashed out

into sunlight like today's
through where maybe that door was—
then slammed it behind her.

Bread, torn for lack of a knife,
and three oranges make
   sufficient picnic
   by the side of the road,
where old stone-cowled wellsprings
and flat concrete modern ones
   congregate in a glade.

Then, while you and our friend
go inspecting new beauties,
   I piss behind a bush
   in the company of *Dracunculus,*
which—to my inexpert eye—
seems to want to be several
different, ill-matched flowers,
   each of them sinister.

Birdsong and goat bells
bring distance closer:
an improvised music—
   or conversation conducted
   in terms of rhythm and pitch—
not easy to grasp or analyse,
   but delicious to listen to.

As preamble to the monastery itself,
we enter Bible-illustration wilderness.
Slopes of haggard boulders frown down at the road,
boulders pitted and fissured, punished-looking,
among which only the toughest of shrubs, the thriftiest thrivers—
a broom in flower now, not making too much of its yellow—
endure what seems a man-hating, saint-haunted place.

So the monastery takes us all the more by surprise
with its prettiness: its garden trim as a marginal
vignette from a Book of Hours, its walls daubed
gorgeously harmonised, *World of Interiors* ochres and creams.
And in the absence of monks—at work, or prayer, presumably—
what a treat to hear bells raised suddenly, untunefully,
in a spasm of clashing, a jam-session
praise-psalm of pots and pans, a no-nonsense
spring cleaning of the air.

That seedcase you picked up and showed me, remember,
  on the tip of your finger?
Like a fractional coin, the mite
  of a mite, dropped and forgotten, and yet
so pleasingly fashioned—spiral
  compact against spiral—
it seemed a talisman, fit emblem of an island
  where labyrinths and lucky finds abound.

Think of the snails, bagged clusters for sale
  in the village shops, that later furnished
part of our feast at that unrecommended
  taverna: twists of griddled succulence
tweaked from their shells with a slack
  twang of reluctance, chewed,
then chased down with a wine
  described on the menu as black.

Or the double conundrum
  of the Phaistos Disc, in Heraklion's
inexhaustible museum: again, a spiral
  front and back, each a centrifugal

procession of hieroglyphs, lyrical enough
    to encourage the thought (unsupported
by scholarship) that it might be a poem.
    No Minotaur, but a flower, at the centre of one of them.

Tordylium, Petromarula,
   love-in-a-mist,
various pea flowers, *Muscari comosum* . . .

Months later, I ask for a list
of the flora invading
the goat-track shortcut
we took to the beach,
   and out it comes with its own
   spontaneous lilt.

(A less objective botanist,
I could add
thistles.)

   All but overgrown,
   the twist and tilt
   of that path above the bay
   permitted a wading,
   occasionally snagged or stumbling,
   single-file progress of two—
   in which, more often than not,
   I followed you.

THE UNFINISHED

1

Sparse breaths, then none—
and it was done.

Listening and hugging hard,
between mouthings
of sweet next-to-nothings
into her ear—
pillow-talk-cum-prayer—
I never heard
the precise cadence
into silence
that argued the end.
Yet I knew it had happened.

Ultimate calm.

Gingerly, as if
loth to disturb it,
I released my arm
from its stiff vigil athwart
that embattled heart
and raised and righted myself,
the better to observe it.

Kisses followed,
to mouth, cheeks, eyelids, forehead,
and a rigmarole
of unheard farewell
kept up as far
as the click of the door.

After six months, or more,
I observe it still.

2

Those last few days
of drug-drowse, coma-comfort,
friends came, if not as many
as before, to keep her company,
to talk, to weep.

At each arriving voice,
I thought I saw
a faint, fleeting
muscular effort
adjust her mouth and jaw
as if in greeting,
as if for a kiss.

But how could that have been?

I talked, too, read aloud
from her favourite Yeats,
or played the last, great
Schubert quartets—
the one in G
that, with whole-hearted
ambivalence,
weighs in the balance

the relative merits
of major and minor
and struggles to postpone the choice.

While I cultivated
my clumsy, husbandly
bedside manner,
she lay as her nurses had arranged her:
reposeful beloved,
stark stranger—
or something in between.

3

'Gently, little boat,
across the ocean float':
Auden's words,
which Stravinsky's ear
slanted, tilted, made more
liltingly awkward.
Out of the whole
ragbag repertoire
of songs she loved to sing,
this lullaby-barcarole
might have been just the thing,
if the bed had been a boat,
and the boat going anywhere.

But, as a wise man said,
'Death is not
an event in life.'
Nor is it a journey.

The hospice bed
bearing my wife
stood in a hushed
back room, moored fast

to the physical facts
of this singular life.
Only in that space
of the mind where the wilful
metaphors thrive
has it now pushed
out into open sea
and begun to travel
beyond time and place,
never to arrive.

4

'Come on, girls,
you can do it!'

The force of the fit
that, after weeks
of merciless paralysis,
shocked her upright,
shouting mad things—
'I can see you
behind that box!'—
frightened me, of course.
Furious as I'd never
known her before
in any of our quarrels,
she was suddenly, somehow,
strong as an ox.
But I held her tight.

'Bastards! Bastards!'

Even now,
theatrical training
lent strength to her lungs

and unmistakable meaning
to this sibylline binge
of gabble, rant and swear words.

A kindly nurse
hurried towards us
with a syringe.

5

No imp or devil
but a mere tumour
squatted on her brain.
Without personality
or ill humour,
malignant but not malign,
it set about doing—
not evil,
simply the job
tumours have always done:
establishing faulty
connections, skewing
perceptions, closing down
faculties and functions
one by one.

Hobgoblin, nor foul fiend;
nor even the jobsworth slob
with a slow, sly scheme to rob
my darling of her mind
that I imagined;
just a tumour.

Between which and the neat
gadget with the timer
that eased drugs into her vein,
she contrived to maintain
her identity
unimpaired and complete,
resolved to meet
death with all gallantry
and distinction.

6

Dead Souls enjoyed
but put aside
midway, *Sense
and Sensibility* done,
she wanted another Austen:
Northanger Abbey.
I brought it in next day.
From the runaway
long first paragraph
onwards, she was happy,
with a staring, intense
involvement and full play
of her relishing laugh
(one faculty not yet affected).

A few sessions in,
we were still in Bath
when she stopped me and said,
'You know, this is so good,
I don't understand
why it's never been written down.'
I held up the book,
reminded her how often

she'd read it before,
argued, grew annoyed,
but nothing shook
that rapt conviction.

So, at her insistence,
in my crabbed hand
I wrote out several sentences,
then some more—
just to be sure
that a great work of comic fiction
would not be forgotten.

7

A warm croissant
and cappuccino
were our morning rite:
alternate bites
of flaking, buttery pith;
then the straw guided
into her mouth
and the coffee making
its hesitant ascent
with puckered sucks
that just as stutteringly subsided.

Tougher work
than playing an oboe,
yet performed with a gusto
that customarily took
more than her fair share.
Not that I was measuring!
Rather, it was a case
of pride and delight
in such simple pleasuring:
the look on her face,
pure, animal appetite.

Therefore, not heartbreaking,
to picture her
across a table
in some quiet French seaside spot,
scanning a cluttered
plateau de fruits de mer
with its full surgical couvert,
and about to clatter
her way through the lot
as slowly as she was able.

8

By good luck, the hospice
was situated
in a foodie haven,
a North London
village-cosmopolis
of delicatessens.

Her first visitors seated,
I was instructed
to run out and find
Żubrówka and Polish
appetisers.
I came back with 'Russian'
vodka, warm,
and *antipasti*.
She seemed not to mind,
and later I got better
at fulfilling such errands
to the letter.

Food and friends,
treats and surprises:
all that she deemed necessary

assumed the tragi-
comic form
of Chekhovian picnics
at our end of the ward,
which she directed, or conducted,
with frail, airy
emphases and flourishes
of her right arm—
the one limb so far spared.

9

How bright the wit,
the circumstance-mocking
theatrical badinage, burned.
To a friend concerned
she might be tired
I heard her say,
'Exhausted people
leave the hospice all day,
and I just carry on talking.'

To another, catching
a glimpse of her own
undimmable spirit:
'I'm being radiant
again, aren't I!'

It was inspired,
brave, funny and subtle
of her to interpret
the role of patient
so flat against type—
cheering her nurses,
feeding advice and support

to friends, encouraging
her husband to address his
possible future
with something of her hope.

It's not in his nature,
but he can try.

10

When the brush had started
tugging out random
tufts and clumps
of springy brown hair
from her outgrown bob,
she asked me to shave
the whole lot off.

Fractious, half-hearted,
I took on the job,
began maladroitly,
then finished it
with a perfectionist's care.

Revealed: a handsome,
unabashed smoothness
I couldn't stop wanting
to fondle and kiss.

Wasn't it something—
that the cup of my hand
and curve of her clean scalp
should turn out to be
such an intimate fit!

The pull to palp
and pamper that round shape,
to learn its lineaments
and feel the hint
of a hint of light stubble
pushing through,
was irresistible.

Virgin landscape,
so neat and so new!

11

So like a baby,
with her bald head
and one working arm
clear of the blanket
that the ambulance men
had folded her in,
but a baby with wide, wise,
learning eyes
and an unexpected
gift of speech,
she proceeded first
to puzzle, then charm
her attendants with a burst
of questions and comments
on everything in reach:
from the gadgets and fixtures
to the colour of her blanket,
a pragmatic scarlet;
then, as the vehicle
speeded along,
the swivelling, wrong-
way-round, receding
view through the window

of just the tops
of houses and shops,
which made a familiar
route hard to follow;
via this, that and the other,
till—how, I can't think—
they were onto the subject
of favourite drinks,
and no one objected
when she nominated
as the most delicious
of all, champagne.

A WIDOWER'S DOZEN

Conundrum

I'm the riddle to an answer:
I'm an unmarried spouse,
a flesh-and-blood revenant,
my own ghost, inhabitant
of an empty house.

A Scattering

I expect you've seen the footage: elephants,
finding the bones of one of their own kind
dropped by the wayside, picked clean by scavengers
and the sun, then untidily left there,
    decide to do something about it.

But what, exactly? They can't, of course,
reassemble the old elephant magnificence;
they can't even make a tidier heap. But they can
hook up bones with their trunks and chuck them
    this way and that way. So they do.

And their scattering has an air
of deliberate ritual, ancient and necessary.
Their great size, too, makes them the very
embodiment of grief, while the play of their trunks
    lends sprezzatura.

Elephants puzzling out
the anagram of their own anatomy,
elephants at their abstracted lamentations—
may their spirit guide me as I place
    my own sad thoughts in new, hopeful arrangements.

Soul

Never having known an emptiness so heavy,
I am inclined to call it my newborn soul,
though its state may be less an achieved birth than a pregnancy
lodged oddly, for lack of a womb, in a tight gap
behind the sternum, mid-thorax, not far from my heart.

Coddled there, it's needy, an energy eater.
It kicks, or thumps, hollowly, and I come to a standstill,
breathless, my whole internal economy primed
to attend without delay to its nursing and nourishment:
memories, sorrows, remorses are what it feeds on.

Luckily, I have no shortage of these to give it,
so that it can continue its murky labours,
quintessential upheavals, noxious bubblings
at the bottom of a flask, as it strives to distil pure tears.

A Reasonable Thing to Ask

Please explain tears.
They must have some purpose
that a Darwin or a Freud
would have understood.

Widowed, a man hears
music off the radio—
Handel—Cole Porter—
that sharply recalls her,
and they swamp up again.

A faculty that interferes
with seeing and speaking
and leaves him feeling weaker:
what does he gain by it?

What do *we* gain by it—
blind to the tiger's leap,
voiceless under the avalanche?
Somebody must know.

Songbook

Songs that used to lift up lightly
 out of the solitude that she occupied:
  where are they now?
Songs that sprang from solitary activity—
 sewing or cooking—but that sought
  and touched my solitude;
songs that elided distance and closeness,
 self-sufficiency and companionship,
  sent out from this room or that
on a wing and a breath of intrepid melody,
 chancing flight from note to note
  through phrases I could tell were relished
for their harmony-implying turns,
 leaping intervals and tricky runs,
  before settling on keynote and silence:
a silence now final and hard to listen to.
 Show tunes, folk tunes, lieder, blues,
  stern laments of the Italian baroque,
meretricious bonbons of pop recalled
 from a wireless-centred fifties childhood:
  a whole unique improbable songbook—
silent, deleted, permanently lost
 as a language or a culture is lost:
  irreparable damage.

Late

Late home one night, I found
she was not yet home herself.
So I got into bed and waited
under my blanket mound,
until I heard her come in
and hurry upstairs.
My back was to the door.
Without turning round,
I greeted her, but my voice
made only a hollow, parched-throated
k-, k-, k- sound,
which I could not convert into words
and which, anyway, lacked
the force to carry.
Nonplussed, but not distraught,
I listened to her undress,
then sidle along the far side
of our bed and lift the covers.
Of course, I'd forgotten she'd died.
Adjusting my arm for the usual
cuddle and caress,
I felt mattress and bedboards

welcome her weight
as she rolled and settled towards me,
but, before I caught her,
it was already too late
and she'd wisped clean away.

Turns

I know it's impossible, but several times
I've heard her calling a greeting
just as she used to, pitching it up
with her own distinctive spin of enquiry
from the first turn of the stairs, as she arrived home.

Once or twice I've been to check; mostly I haven't.
I know she's dead and I don't believe in ghosts,
nor that the house has been saving up
old echoes as rationed treats and rewards.
It's my brain, that's all, turned whimsically ventriloquist.

I'm still taken in by its craftiness, its know-how.
With its psychotechnological sleight-of-sound, it does
what I can't do: summon up
her loved voice, perfect in pitch, timbre and inflection.
A variety turn—that never fails to give me a turn.

Bathroom of the Vanities

The model mask, the mannequin moue,
the face I loved to catch her pulling
after sundry perfecting dabs
and micro-adjustments in front of the mirror
will never be seen, by me or the mirror, again.

The bathroom scales, too,
stand abandoned. No one now will be consulting
the age-fogged dial for its little fibs
and trembles of error
with precisely that peering-downward frown.

Odd bottles in an orderly queue—
Issey Miyake, *Parfum Tea Rose*, the eternally billing
doves of *L'Air du Temps*—keep their caps
on, conserve their last drops of essence and aura
and wait for no one.

Flowers in Wrong Weather

Snowdrops, crocuses and hellebore,
which last year must have done their shy, brave thing
unobserved by me, are out again this year.

I was in the garden bagging
tree trash the gales had flung down the week before.
No gardener, even I could tell the job needed doing.

Now it was a too-mild February morning.
The flowers looked misplaced, without some ice in the air
or bullying wind to give them their full meaning.

Or was it just that there was nobody to share
the annual miracle with? Crocuses piercing
the soil with a palpable pang; the dear

droop of snowdrops; hellebore
stoically averted: all missing the welcome and blessing
of the one who had planted them there.

About the House

The fragment of rusted, possibly agricultural metal
that she found when digging and that became
Mother and Child, without the Child;

the elongated Wapping-mudlarked flint
that, from its tilt when stood on end, got called
Russian Peasant Woman Walking through a Snowstorm—

these and suchlike trouvailles-turned-knickknacks
keep their place about the house, though symbolically inert now,
their only function to be a bother to the cleaner with her duster.

Nevertheless, they will stay there until a decision has been
    announced
by the Senior Curator, Department of Private Jokes.

Exasperated Piety

Majestically indignant, Henry James
    in his preface to *The Altar of the Dead*—
paragraphs I have read and reread—
    cites instances, but forbears to name names,
as he recalls the gross metropolitan snub
    whereby old friends and associates who had died
were not so much forgotten as denied:
    a frosty ostracism from the club
of the left-over living. I paraphrase crudely
    James's pained, feeling and reasoning prose,
but I, too, have met the tribal will to impose
    taboos and codes, and have behaved rudely,
invoking my dead wife in dinner-table conversation.
    A beat of silence, of shared fear and sick shock, falls,
a symptom of the malaise that James himself calls
    'the awful doom of general dishumanisation'.
He blamed London: 'a terrible place to die in';
    'the poor dead, all about one, were nowhere so dead as there.'
I see an old writer, gagging on the ghost-rich air
    of a fashionable salon, a terrible place to cry in.

An Italian Market

A market: a mêlée
mainly of women,
a bargain-driven, midweek bacchanale.

I have come not to buy
but to look, to spy,
as they scrum around stalls heaped with salads of fabric,

chatting and chaffering, scooping
and fingering goods, comparing
qualities, holding flaws up to the light.

If they don't know quite
what they want, they know
what they don't want, and they're much too busy,

too attuned to a powerful purpose,
to notice the undisguised voyeur
who has come there to sneak a taste

of the strong, health-giving, world-immersed
feminine element
his life has lacked for too long.

Afterlife

As if she couldn't bear not to be busy and useful
after her death, she willed her body to medical science.

Today, as a number of times before, I walked
past the institution that took her gift, and thought,

'That's where my dead wife lives. I hope they're treating her
kindly.'

The dark brick, the depthless windows, gave nothing away,
but the place seemed preferable to either Heaven or Hell,

whose multitudes meekly receive whatever the design teams
and PR whizzes of religion have conjured up for them.

My wife is in there, somewhere, doing practical work:
her organs and tissues are educating young doctors

or helping researchers outwit the disease that outwitted her.
So it's a hallowed patch of London for me now.

But it's not a graveyard, to dawdle and remember and mope in,
and I had work to do, too, in a different part of town.

LUCINDA'S WAY

Having had the good fortune to live in the *roman-fleuve*
of your life, my darling,
playing no small part, but—that's not my name on the cover—
second always to you, the dashing heroine,
I have hesitated, havered too long, to compose
this necessary footnote.
You would have understood why.

I write now in the cumbersome
retrospective mood;
you lived in the present future,
a tense of your own invention.

The text hurtled along. There was no time for revision.
Unpublished, a dozen different, variant manuscripts,
distributed among friends, who refer to them frequently.
My own copy is in front of me this minute.
This way and that, I turn the exhilarating pages.
Exhilarating and sad.

Did anyone ever match your appetite
for plans and projects,
for doing two or three things at the same time?

You watched bad television, had me massage your neck and
    sewed
lavishly beautiful patchwork quilts.

When that quack put you on a punishing diet,
you pedalled a borrowed exercise bicycle
for however many static miles a day
and learned Italian from a book supported on the handlebars.

Your breakfast reading was a gardening encyclopaedia
which took up half the table;
you absorbed the Linnaean taxonomy along with your
    grapefruit and coffee.

Two or three things at the same time.
Can't you now somehow contrive
to be both dead and alive?

Jealous of the years when I didn't know you,
I interrogate the documentary evidence:
photographs, diaries and notebooks, letters home
that your mother saved up and in due course
bundled and returned.
Now, sadly, I own them.

More than once, you wondered if I would have liked
the you of those days. Meeting her too late, I love her
with a futile fervour.

Against advice, you had left South Africa
for a London fondly constructed from old books and high
    hopes,
to enlist in the rackety acting profession.
RADA accepted you. You attended classes. Made friends.
Splurged on adventurous recipes for dinner parties
but, totting up the pennies in the ruled back pages of a pocket
    diary,
survived the rest of the week
on cashew nuts and packet soup.

You went to shows; sewed your own clothes; were elated
and disappointed.

You lived at such speed that the ballpoint script
running aslant and fading
across the faded blue
can scarcely keep up. Many words are illegible. I miss
important steps. Your movements blur. I want to follow, but can't.

The theatre is a big, ramshackle, blindly trundling machine.
With bits falling off it, it clatters through the generations,
more wasteful of lives than a losing army.

You fed it your love and it gave you too little in return.

I retain visions of you in a number of costumes—
many times washed but still fusty, scuffed shiny, resewn—
playing Wilde, Ibsen, Shaw, Kaufman and Hart . . .
The stage lit a different gaudiness for each one.

You are a wronged wife, stately and angry. You are a fluffy
    secretary.
You are prim. You are passionate. You weep. You argue. You
    laugh.

Controlled, melodious, your voice rises up
from you through your character
and reaches into the large, listening darkness,
where I sit and hear again
the lines I helped you to learn.

Watching was like being with you, closer than a stalker,
shadowing both the blocked moves

and the unrehearsed gestures,
present when you thrust and parried in a passage of witticisms,
when you turned your back in scorn, when you yielded and
  kissed.
(That was hard for a husband!)

But I never saw you in either Shakespeare or Chekhov,
your two great loves.
I never saw you in the parts they wrote for you. Nobody did.

Brave trade: to step into that box of brightness
and be someone utterly else. An object. An opposite.

Is that why actors are so routinely mocked and reviled?
Scapegoats for their scapegrace lives
as enigmatic as those of the Gipsies,
and their lore as recondite as the Jews',
they subscribe to a function both sacramental and frivolous,
transcendent and transitory.

Second-hand glory,
but I was proud
to be married to one of the tribe.

A marriage and its legends.
Stories told once, found good,
then warmed up on occasion
to confirm the sanctity
of a secular union.

This from prehistory,
the age of Joan Baez
and wafty cheesecloth dresses:
you were draped neck to toe in white
and crossing a London street—
I wish I'd asked you which one—
when the little oracular boy
who always passes by
exclaimed, 'Look! Daddy! A ghost!'

Jokes, too. Each time you brought out
the ugly passport photo
that showed you flash-pallid and gawping
in some dingy, tube-station booth,
I said, 'A ghost that's seen a ghost.'

A story and a poor joke
that have lately adjusted their meaning
to an unbearable truth.

A Faust moment.
Not as ghost
but as true presence,
willed piecemeal
from memory fragments,
you step towards me
in full rig,
unmistakable at a distance.

Sprung, affirmative poise.
Head slightly tilted.
Discernible mariner's sway,
as if your foothold
on terra firma
were less than secure—
as it turned out to be.

You're wearing homemade
Turkish trousers,
one of your fearlesss
unfashion statements;
shirt loose as a tunic;

wild hair bunched
in an ikat bandanna,
for extra buccaneer effect.

The sensitive lenses
of your big, strong spectacles
have darkened in the sunlight
I have prepared for you,
and you are smiling
an undimmed hello.
So everything is all right.

Wobble. Dissolve.

You wanted the garden to be a plenty, a plenitude:
no barbered-to-baldness parsimony of lawn
with flowers and shrubs pushed to the edge, attendant
like hired staff at a heartless banquet.
So it is now, though without doubt more anarchic,
through my neglect, than you had in mind.

Approaching midsummer, roses shoot everywhere.
Tangled arches ambitiously aspire, but are weighed down,
it seems, by the sheer fatness
of clusters of blooms all manner of white and off-white,
lolling into the gardens on either side. Nobody has
    complained.

The iris you planted next to the rosemary—*Iris orientalis*—
put on its best performance yet two weeks ago,
and even its present tatters manage a certain panache.
Astrantia in the shade of the quince tree looks brisk and sturdy.
Solanum continues to hoist itself
by stealth from bush to bush.
Your disappointing honeysuckle has tried hard, while the
    abutilon

remains steady.
Then there are all the flowers I don't know the names of:
crowd-fillers, walk-ons . . .

Paths we laid with fragments of kangoed Yorkstone
are smothered, forget where they're going—but who cares?

Genius of growth and overgrowth, you planned this small
London back plot
to be where a gardener, a lone Eve, could lose herself utterly.
When I came out to call you in to supper,
or to the pestering telephone,
often you seemed to have vanished until I spotted you
bent over or squatting in the midst of some urgent green
    handiwork.
Lost to sight for a different reason, you're still to be found there
if I look carefully.

The documents are gathered, assorted, stored.

Archivist of box files and shoe boxes,
like a miser I lift to the light and count
treasure I own but cannot spend.
This currency has been withdrawn from circulation.

Among the too few photographs of you,
your self-effacing self-portraits
pierce me with their dandyish nonchalance.
(And why can't a woman be a dandy?)
Mirrors, shop windows, reflective surfaces of any kind,
served for these studies in the erasure of identity.
The very means of recording became your mask;
your hair, your hats, your clothes, your confronting stance—
like an exclamation mark conveyed *sotto voce*—
the signs by which you are known.
Sometimes you have your husband by your side,
a vague, off-centre presence.

Old doors were another subject you favoured:
eloquently weathered but taciturn
as to what lay behind them.

Memories. Weighty emptinesses. I live in a memory
the size and shape of a house.

Such was my luck that, lacking religion, you gave your ardour
to customs, ceremonies, graces
of a domestic order.

Shopping list, phone message, birthday-present label,
proxy greeting left on the kitchen table:
you told me you never threw away a scrap of my writing
without kissing it first.

When we sold the flat we had lived in for—amazingly—
    seventeen years,
you visited our few small rooms in turn
and out loud said goodbye to the empty spaces.

One afternoon, years later, we crossed on the stairs.
Unprompted, you announced, 'I love our house'—
an outburst of the plainest happiness
that the high stairwell
enshrines still.

While the innumerable air kisses
we exchanged in passing
remain suspended to this day,
each one an efficacious blessing.

ANNIVERSARY

(2015)

Anniversary

No more fervent celebrant than you
of birthdays, anniversaries and feasts
that broke the humdrum of the year, demanding
ceremony, gifts and merrymaking.

Our six privately sacred days
came round, came round and round again,
but, when your death fell a fortnight short of your birthday,
failed to complete the cycle, their twenty-ninth.
Instead, an anniversary was added
to my year, if not to yours.

Now the tenth approaches; and it will pass
without ceremony, without merriment.
But an exchange of gifts should still be possible:
poems from me to you, the memories
of which they are made
from you to me.

The Lion of Lemnos

Who pushed the tumbler?
I can't believe it was you,
neither of our guests
looked the likely culprit,
and it certainly wasn't me.
No, we were in earnest—
well-boozed but in earnest—
as the upturned glass,
uncommonly roused and headstrong,
slid, paused, edged away,
hesitated and pounced
from letter to letter
in answer to our questions.

We had got through
to a certain Miss Lomax—
first name, dates of birth and death
undisclosed—
but speaking to us,
albeit with difficulty,
from somewhere in the middle
of the eighteenth century.
She wanted to tell us

about the Lion of Lemnos,
some old wrong, or shady business,
or misunderstanding
concerning it and the British Museum.
But what, precisely?

She couldn't, or wouldn't, explain,
however hard we pressed her;
our pestering flustered her
and threw her into deeper
and more frequent silences;
we had lost her attention, her trust,
and she was withdrawing.
What put it into your head then
to ask her about next Saturday's
lottery numbers?
I remonstrated. Our friends laughed.
The game was over.
Diffident Miss Lomax
and her mysterious Lion
had fled, to remain—with you now—
unreachable on the far side.

Lucipher

The name we went by
when we shared an address
@compuserve.
You thought of it.

Straight away, I
adored its wit,
its mischief, its nerve,
its mongrelness.

In a word, we became—
for each other—
a marriage myth
of the cybersphere.

Then you died, and with
much administrative bother
and wear and tear
I forsook the name.

The Language of Love

1

Mon poux,
contraction of *mon époux*:
endearment.
Louse for spouse!
From the topsy-turvy
language of love.
Mon p'tit poux:
the two *ps* making
a quickfire double kiss.
Thank you. Thank you.

2

Tu es une ange!
But *ange* is masculine
and you loved French too much
to let me get away
with such a solecism.
So I repeated it often,
as I do today
addressing you,
unmasculine angel!

Our Daughter

Our scary teenage daughter
still hangs by a butcher's hook
through her topknot of ribbons
from the end of the bookcase.

Punk rag doll
of the zany, spacy, stitchwork eyes
and goth-black smirk,
she is used to being ignored.

Guests come and go—
otherwise talkative folk,
who haven't a word to say
either about her or to her.

Might it be the way she's dressed:
miniest of miniskirts,
lace-topped stockings, mismatched,
those trinkets and baubles?

Or her attitude, perhaps?
The taunt of her little, bare paunch?
Dumb insolence, hard to distinguish
from dumb appeal?

Dumbness must be catching!
No matter, social life
proceeds without her;
and she, ostentatiously, without it.

Effigy only child,
same age as when I gave her to you
as a wedding-anniversary present—
our twenty-first.

Lobsters

Kind Tom Lynch
gave us his cottage
in West Clare,
free of charge:
the ideal base
from which to launch
breezy forays
along that spectacular,
wind-assailed coast
and inland across
the austere, riven
karst plateau of the Burren.
Generous days!

And a generous evening
when Seamus and Marie
drove from Dublin
to dine with us.
'Brine-stung glut'
not far from my mind,
we obtained, not oysters,
but enormous lobsters
from the hatchery,

only to find
as they simmered in their pot
that our kitchen lacked
apparatus
to open them with.

No worries:
here was a hammer!
Passing it around,
we stooped to the stone floor
and whacked and whacked
at the samurai armour
with relish, with flair.
Feasting and mirth;
the laying down
of an unofficial memory;
what such times are for.

Amazonian

Isabel Godin des Odonais and you
met in a footnote
to Prescott's *History of the Conquest of Peru.*

It was identification at first sight,
and you started a play
such as nobody else would think to try to write.

It began with a song:
an Amazonian creation myth
made up by yourself and twenty-seven verses long.

Unfriendly Indians formed a Greek chorus
commenting on the party
of doomed European travellers you'd assembled for us.

Mme Godin was to be sole survivor,
but the expedition never got going.
Instead: pages and pages of typescript showing

all the research you'd done,
a jungle of data. How I wish you'd managed to put
her brave, three-thousand-mile journey on the stage;

and her husband there to welcome her
as she arrived,
distressed, in tatters and barefoot,

at the mouth of the Amazon.

Auf dem Wasser zu singen

A certain landscape always got you going:
soft hills or downland, and the road ahead
amiably meandering out of sight.

At the wheel, some impulse of delight
would prompt a verse or two of Schubert's flowing,
6/8 melody. Now that you're dead,

Irmgard Seefried on CD must do instead,
though she can never hope to rival quite
your pitch of joy, windows wound down, breeze blowing.

One Night Only

Too few saw you in your last theatre rôle,
the affected hero of *La Forêt mouillée*,
Victor Hugo's seldom-performed verse play.
Cross-dressed, in whiteface, top hat and cutaway—
from my late father's wardrobe—you stole the show.

No, that's not it; that wasn't your style; you simply took
rightful possession of the part,
learnt pages of alexandrines off by heart,
flew to rehearsals in Provence and, fired
by months of Bernard's coaching and coaxing, acquired
the voice, gestures, gait and look that he desired,
and became, for one night only, *comédienne*.

Not *comédien*. Nobody in the hall
could have mistaken you for a man,
though, equally, nobody doubted you were French.
This being a Bernard production, the cast
included Indian dancers, opera singers, the village choir,
a vast ensemble, less theatre than carnival—
and starring you! You surpassed
even yourself. It was your most sublime performance
and your last.

Two Commands

Among the wise things you said
from your banked and raised hospice bed
were two commands to me.
One: that I should be
less inclined to procrastinate.
(Shameful to relate,
I promised I would—but not yet.)
The second, that I should get
married again,
shocked and silenced me then;
yet I am happily married now,
as happily as I was,
and no doubt largely because
you showed me how
such happiness can be sought,
found, caught,
and kept by a shared will
through fortunes both good and ill,
or the mixture and muddle between.
You would know what I mean.

Printed in the USA
CPSIA information can be obtained
at www.ICGtesting.com
LVHW010341150724
785510LV00002B/219

9 780374 538088